Barbara Persing

Listen to Your Quilt

Select the Perfect Quilting Every Time

4 Simple Steps

D1509700

PUBLISHING

Text copyright © 2012 by Barbara Persing

Photography and Artwork copyright © 2012 by C&T Publishing, Inc.

Publisher: Amy Marson

Creative Director: Gailen Runge

Editor: Deb Rowden

Technical Editor: Teresa Stroin

Cover Designer: April Mostek

Book Designer: Kerry Graham

Page Layout Artist: Casey Dukes

Production Coordinator: Zinnia Heinzmann

Production Editors: Alice Mace Nakanishi and S. Michele Fry

Illustrators: Mary E. Flynn and Jessica Jenkins

Photography by Christina Carty-Francis and Diane Pedersen of C&T Publishing, Inc., unless otherwise noted.

Published by C&T Publishing, Inc., P.O. Box 1456, Lafayette, CA 94549

Library of Congress Cataloging-in-Publication Data

Persing, Barbara, 1962-

Listen to your quilt : select the perfect quilting every time : 4 simple steps / Barbara Persing.

   p. cm.

ISBN 978-1-60705-500-6 (soft cover)

1. Machine quilting. 2. Machine quilting--Patterns. I. Title.

TT835.P449124 2012

746.46'041--dc23

                          2011034029

Printed in China

10 9 8 7 6 5 4 3 2 1

Dedication

I dedicate this book to:

My best friend

My complementary puzzle piece

My inspiration

My reality check

The one who can read my mind

The one I can have an entire conversation with through just one look

The one I owe my success to

My sister

Mary Hoover

Acknowledgments

Writing a book takes a village! And I am very blessed to have a great village. I need to thank my husband of 30 years, Paul. He has been my cheerleader, champion, and friend from the very beginning. Where did those 30 years go? We've had so much fun! And to my sons, Kyle and Quinn, who brighten my world—you are very patient and know more about quilting than most men. I love you.

To the C&T family—for being so supportive, encouraging, and talented. You are a joy to work with, and you make the daunting task of writing a book less overwhelming. Your expertise and experience are beyond measure.

To my mom—for the beautiful example she sets as a mother and friend, for teaching me to sew, and for giving me the best friends and support group I will ever have—my siblings, Ann, Kathy, Jeanne, Michael, and Mary.

To my clients—without whom I would not be the quilter I am today—you have supported me and challenged me to be my best. Thank you for allowing me to collaborate on all your beautiful quilts.

Thank you all for being part of my village.

Contents

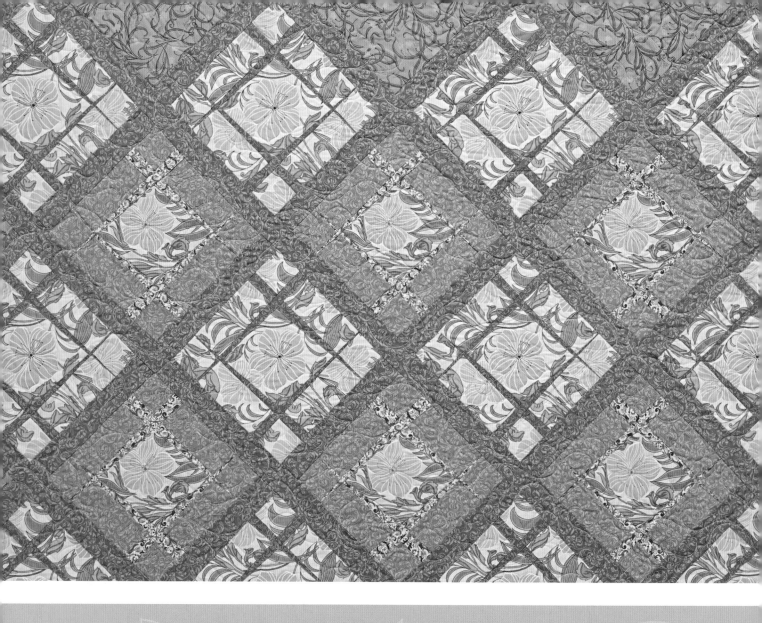

Introduction

As soon as the piecework is done and your quilt top is finished, does panic set in? Do you ask yourself, "How should I quilt this quilt?" No matter what technique we use—domestic machine, longarm machine, or hand quilting—we all face the same question. My years as a longarm quilter have helped me find a unique approach for choosing the best quilting designs. It's simple and straightforward, and everyone can implement it.

Every time I am ready to begin quilting, I ask myself the same four questions. By answering these questions, I have a clear idea of how I want to quilt any quilt and which thread to use. This book will take you through these steps and show you how to apply this knowledge to your quilts.

All of the quilting ideas in this book are created free motion and require no marking tools. Most of these designs can also be done in a continuous line. Whether you are looking for simple allover designs or custom heirloom quilting, you will find plenty of ideas in this book.

So read on and begin to master your quilting *design* skills.

Developing Your Quilting Skills

My Path

I did not start my career as a longarm quilter. Like most people, I have had a number of careers, and only due to circumstance and persistence did I end up here. In the early years of my marriage, my husband and I lived in New Hampshire. I worked as a respiratory therapist for six years and enjoyed my work very much. We then had the opportunity to move back to the Philadelphia area and be close to our families. Even though I had enjoyed my previous career, I decided to make a change and went to work for a large group of orthopedic surgeons. I helped them establish a new practice, and I managed the daily office operations. This job was challenging and always changing. However, during the years I worked for them, I started a family and was looking for another change. I wanted a job that would allow me to be home with my young family.

I suggested to my husband that I resign my position, start my own business, and buy a really big quilting machine—a longarm machine. He was a little skeptical but gave me all of his support. That was in May of 2000, and I have been running my longarm machine quilting business ever since.

To keep me on my toes, my sister Mary Hoover and I then formed a partnership and started our own pattern company, Fourth and Sixth Designs. We also wrote a book, *StrataVarious Quilts*, published by C&T Publishing.

Luckily, I have had the pleasure of sharing these jobs with my sister. She is an excellent partner who, like me, has an obsession with quilting.

I had convinced my husband about this new career and about buying this big quilting machine, but there was one concern: *I did not machine quilt!* Even though I had been making quilts as a hobby, I had never machine quilted. I had always hand quilted the tops and didn't know a lot about machine quilting. So I did my research, went to local quilt shows, and tried out all the longarm machines. I talked to anyone who knew anything about the machines and chose the machine that I thought best suited my purposes.

I ordered my machine and was so eager for delivery that I started making quilt tops. I also had Mary piecing tops in New York. I needed many pieced quilt tops on which to practice before venturing onto clients' quilts. My machine was delivered and set up in my home, and then I had about two hours of instruction before *the machine representative left.* Wait a minute—I was *on my own!?*

Like most longarm quilters, I first learned to quilt using pantograph designs. A pantograph design is a quilting design drawn on a long roll of paper that you follow with a laser pointer.

Pantograph design

Pantograph designs are quilted as you stand in the back of the machine; you do not face the quilt. This means the quilting is done with no regard to the piecework.

Working from the back of the machine

Following the pantograph designs taught me how to control the motion of my machine and how to be consistent with speed and stitch length. All of this is a very important part of getting comfortable with a longarm machine.

I had practiced and was now ready for clients. I looked forward to starting my new business and leaving behind all day-to-day decision making that came with office management. I thought that when I received quilts, my customers would tell me how they wanted their quilts quilted. My first client came to my house and showed me her quilt; when I asked how she wanted it quilted, she said, "I don't know. You're the expert." I didn't see that coming. I thought customers would make all the quilting decisions, and I would do the quilting. Machine quilting was fairly new to me, so I just chose the best pantograph design. After a couple of months of using pantographs, however, I found that this redundant quilting process was losing its challenge. After learning all those pantograph designs, I discovered this was not going to be the path for me. Instead, I wanted to see the quilt and create designs that better complemented my customers' work. So I moved to the front of my machine.

Working from the front of the machine

Practice, Practice, Practice

If you are learning to quilt on a domestic machine or a longarm machine, practice is the only way to get better at what you do. You don't need to use a pantograph design to get started, but you should start quilting with simple and easy designs.

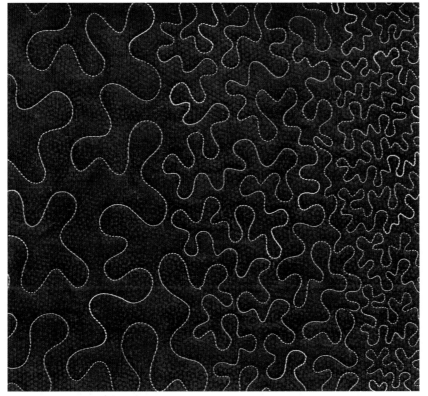

Stippling in different scales—large to small

Loops

Get to know everything about your sewing machine. Learn how to use your domestic or longarm machine for quilting and how to prepare your quilt for your particular machine. Keeping your machine in good working order will require you to be very familiar with the owner's manual. Learn about tension and thread types and how each behaves on your machine (see Types of Thread, page 17).

It is difficult to learn two skills at one time—that is, the physical part of quilting and the mental part of designing. You need to be comfortable with the speed and motion of the machine. As you quilt, you are building muscle memory, which means you are teaching your body a new motion.

Some people quilt with their machine running fast, and some people quilt with their machine running slow. Not everyone is the same, and there is no wrong way. You need to quilt at a speed that gives you a consistent stitch length. Your machine speed will vary depending on the difficulty of the design. As with any other skill, practice makes perfect. Practice your quilting on simple projects with simple designs to build your confidence. If your first projects are too difficult, you will quickly become frustrated and think, "I can't do this." We all have to start somewhere. Remember that those award-winning quilts you see at quilt shows were done by someone who started her first quilt with a simple design.

Eventually your quilting skill will become second nature, and this activity of machine quilting will become automatic. Then you will not need the same amount of concentration and focus that you applied when you were a beginner.

By practicing with simple designs, you give yourself the chance to learn a physical skill as well as a mental skill. The goal is to make the physical part of quilting a skill that you can do without too much thought so you can focus on the design aspects. Just as you can now write without thinking about how each letter is made, you want to be able to quilt without having to think about each movement. When the simple designs, such as loops, become second nature, you can then build on them by adding other motifs, such as flowers, leaves, and stars.

Loops and daisies

Loops and leaves

Loops and stars

Loops as ribbon candy

Loops in sashing

You can change your loops into a more uniform design, such as a line of loops. Because you are now familiar with this shape, you can transition easily to changes in the design. You can even make loops in sashing and borders.

You will be surprised at how quickly you become comfortable with new designs. The possibilities will expand, and you will start to create your own motifs. Quilting is like doodling on paper, only you are doing it on your quilt. Some people practice new designs on paper, but I find I am better at creating new designs on my machine—my paper drawings are not nearly as good as my quilting. Look at the design motifs in your fabrics to see what you can make into quilting designs (see the detail image of *Oh So Sweet*, page 19).

Free-Motion Quilting

Free-motion quilting is done using no patterns and no computer-guided machines. You guide the machine and create the quilting designs as you go. On a longarm machine, this is when you quilt from the front of the machine and work facing the quilt. I like to see the quilt and be more involved with how the finished quilt will look.

Initially I was more comfortable with quilting allover designs. I created quilting designs inspired by the fabrics in the quilt, and then I would repeat those designs as an allover quilting design.

Fabric

Quilting design inspired by fabric, in different scales—small to large

Moving on to Custom Quilting

What Is "Custom" Quilting?

Any quilting that is not done as an allover design is custom quilting. Custom quilting involves choosing quilting designs to fit each area on the quilt—for example, borders, sashing, and blocks. Custom quilting does not have to be densely quilted, but it will always be quilting that is designed specifically for each part of the quilt. Custom quilting can have many thread stops and starts, but it is possible to plan your designs so you can move from one design to the next in a continuous line.

This is my favorite type of quilting. I like to look at a quilt and see it in all of its individual pieces, just as the quilter did when she began her project. Seeing the quilt this way helps me connect to the quilt and share in the quilter's vision. Rather than using an allover design, I fill the spaces—the individual blocks of a four-patch, the triangles in a Flying Geese design, or the borders and sashing in a quilt. Look at *Birdhouse* (page 32), for example. Many times, I can now continue from one area of design to another without breaking the thread for a stop and start. (For ideas, see Quilting Designs, pages 58–69.) With a little practice, you too can learn how to do all this as continuous line and custom quilting at the same time.

Sometimes the custom quilting can only be done with many stops and starts; for example, *The Sampler* (page 44) has a border, appliqué, and background that were all quilted with designs created to fill each individual space. When you choose to do this type of custom quilting, sometimes referred to as *heirloom quilting*, you have to realize the extensive time commitment you are making. This is the type of custom quilting that you want to work up to.

Enhancing the Quilt with Quilting

Now that you are comfortable with your machine and quilting, it is time to move on to making good design choices for your quilts.

When I am deciding how to quilt a quilt, I want to make it the best I can. I work for a variety of quilters with varied interests, which means I see many different styles of quilts. This adds to the challenge. I need to relate to each quilt and let it tell me how it should be quilted. This is when I "let the quilt speak," which takes focus and a lot of new ideas.

Ideas are funny things. They come at different times and not necessarily the moment I need them. I would love to look at a quilt and have the perfect idea the second I see it, but that is not always the way it works. Sometimes I have to think about a quilt for a while. Other times I will know one design I want to use and where I want to use it, so I will start there, often without knowing how I am going to complete the quilting. But as I begin to quilt, my mind relaxes, and I can think about the rest of the quilt. The same will happen to you, and you will be surprised by the ideas you get.

Beginning a quilt without knowing the entire plan may be disconcerting, but as you read through the following chapters, you will see how to build on your quilting motifs and discover which designs work best together. You will soon have a full arsenal of designs to choose from.

How Much Quilting?

There has been much discussion on the topic of how much to quilt. Now that machine quilting is so popular, some wonder whether we get carried away with the amount of quilting. One of the most frequent comments I hear is, "Why did she put so much quilting on that quilt?" or "Why doesn't the quilting seem to go with that quilt?" As machine quilting has become acceptable, quilters have been adding dense, tight quilting to everything. And if you go to quilt shows, you may think that all the show winners have very dense quilting. In most cases, these quilts were designed with this type of quilting in mind. But these examples of quilting are only one type of quilt—a show quilt—and that type of quilting does not apply to every quilt.

The amount of quilting on your quilt is a personal choice. Some people like more, and some like less. The goal is to find the proper balance. Remember, it is your quilt, and you get to decide!

Rules

Quilting is a form of self-expression, and as such, it doesn't need rules. Rule are necessary in many places. For example, I have rules at home—but I am raising two children, and, without rules, there is conflict. For quilting, however, following good *guidelines* will help you be technically better. If you already have a method that works for you and that achieves the same result, stay with your method. There are no rules in quilting.

Four Steps to Choosing the Best Quilting

Each quilt starts with the same question: *How am I going to quilt this quilt?* After you answer the following four questions, you should have a clear idea of your quilting plan.

1. **What is the category of this quilt?**

2. **What is the intended use of this quilt?**

3. **What quilting is needed to enhance this quilt?**

4. **What thread color should I use?**

As with any job, a good system of organization and a linear train of thought will help get the job done. Any task that you repeat day to day will become easier because you begin to modify your approach to the task, making yourself more efficient. A good example is something as simple as grocery shopping. I am sure you have a method to your madness—and you probably don't even realize it. You have decided which store you go to, what time of day you shop, and which aisle you start in.

This works the same for quilting. Because I quilt every day, I need to be efficient while still getting the best results. Without even realizing it, I began to follow the same thought process for each quilt. As clients came to drop off their quilts, I would ask them the same questions that I was asking myself: What category does this quilt fit into? What is the intended use of the quilt? What quilting is needed to enhance the quilt? What thread color should I use?

Many quilters don't think they can choose the best quilting or don't think they know enough to choose. They often say, "I don't have any idea what to put on this quilt." But as we start to discuss their quilt, they *do* know what they like and what they don't like, and that is half the battle.

STEP 1
Determine the Category of the Quilt

I use the following four categories. Yes, there are many more categories of quilts, but for our purposes, this is all we need.

- Children's/youth quilt

- Traditional quilt

- Contemporary quilt

- Art quilt

Knowing the category of the quilt helps me decide what type of quilting designs I might use. For example, on a traditional quilt, I might choose designs such as feathers, crosshatching, stippling, or echoing. For a contemporary or art quilt, I might create designs that are angular or irregular or that are inspired by the quilt. Some designs are used in many quilt categories; it is just a matter of how you use them. See the examples in the later chapters of this book: Children's/Youth Quilts (page 18), Traditional Quilts (page 25), Contemporary Quilts (page 35), and Art Quilts (page 47).

Your initial impression of the quilt will tell you what category the quilt belongs in. *The two most important influences that determine category are color and fabric choices.* These two design elements will give you much information. On pages 12 and 13 are examples of how color and fabric can define a quilt's category.

Both of these quilts were made using the same traditional block. However, I would put the tan quilt in the traditional category and the orange quilt in the contemporary category. My impression of these two quilts is solely influenced by the colors used. As you can see, each quilt was quilted in a completely different fashion. *Tan Pumpkin Seed* has echo quilting between each appliqué piece, and its border is an equally balanced heirloom feather design. *The Sampler* has many different quilting designs throughout. The quilting motifs vary widely, and there is no set pattern to where they are placed. The quilting on the border of *The Sampler* has four different design elements, each running into the other. Had the quilting of the two been reversed, neither quilt would have had the correct look.

Remember, even though we are using categories, some quilts will cross boundaries. Also, some quilts are made and used for business purposes, such as a shop sample, pattern cover, or booth display. But for our purposes, we are just trying to find a starting point to help us decide how to quilt a quilt.

Tan Pumpkin Seed

Detail of quilting

The Sampler

Detail of quilting

Children's/Youth Quilts

- Crib quilts

- Quilts for children or teenagers

- Bright fabric, '30s prints, pastels

See the chapter featuring children's and youth quilts (page 18).

Traditional Quilts

- Quilts with traditional blocks, such as Nine-Patches, Sawtooth Stars, Drunkard's Path

- Traditional settings for blocks, such as straight set, blocks on point, sashing, borders

- Appliqué quilts with traditional fabrics

- Fabrics such as calicoes, florals, reproduction prints, muted tones

See the chapter featuring traditional quilts (page 25).

Contemporary Quilts

- Unusual quilt design or block settings

- Appliqué using bright and unusual fabrics

- Fabrics such as batiks, bright bold colors, large-scale florals

See the chapter featuring contemporary quilts (page 35).

Art Quilts

- Pictorial quilts

- Painted quilts

- Abstract-style quilts

- Many types of fabrics in one quilt, such as hand-painted cottons, silks, broadcloth, dyed, and woven fabrics

See the chapter featuring art quilts (page 47).

STEP 2
Determine the Intended Use of the Quilt

- Children's/youth quilt

- Bed quilt

- Wall quilt

- Show quilt / family heirloom

Why is this important? It will help you decide how much quilting you are going to do and where to begin to focus your thoughts for design choices.

Children's/youth quilts   These quilts are going to be used every day and washed frequently, so you want to choose quilting that won't *break your heart* when it starts to show wear. An even density of quilting will hold the batting in place after many washings. I generally use allover quilting designs or custom designs that are not complicated and don't require too many stops and starts.

Bed quilts   There are varying degrees of use for quilts in this category, and that degree will help determine how much quilting you want to do. Some special quilts are gently used, so you may want to add custom or heirloom quilting. Other quilts will be used every day, so you may want to quilt with an allover or partial custom quilting design.

Wall quilts   These quilts are going to be viewed like art. Because of the intended use of the quilt, the quilting will play an important role. It is necessary to choose quilting that enhances the quilt and adds viewing interest. You will want to plan custom quilting by taking into consideration separate block and border treatments, by planning quilting motifs for open spaces, and by paying special attention to appliqué.

Show quilts / family heirlooms   The quilting must be as exceptional as the quilt design. Even if the quilting is not the main focus, these quilts will have a significant amount of quilting and a specific quilting plan. You will want to balance your quilting motifs and possibly mark some quilting lines. These quilts typically have many thread color changes to specifically match or complement the fabrics.

STEP 3
Brainstorm What Quilting Is Needed to Enhance the Quilt

- Allover quilting

- Partial custom quilting

- Full custom quilting

- Heirloom quilting

The goal is to decide what type of quilting is needed on your quilt. This can be the quickest question to answer or the longest. Take your time and think about the other questions asked in this chapter. And remember—knowing the quilt's use will help point you in the right direction.

Here is a brief description of the four types of quilting I refer to in this book.

Allover quilting   Usually done as continuous line quilting. The quilting lines pay no attention to the piecework, as in *Blue* (page 26).

Partial custom quilting   Uses some of the spaces created by the piecework as a guideline for quilting and then uses an allover design on the rest of the quilt, as in *Bliss* (page 27).

Full custom quilting   Uses all the spaces created by the piecework as a guideline for quilting, as in *Trip Around the World* (page 34).

Heirloom quilting   Dense quilting that is no more than ¼" apart and that pays close attention to all the spaces created by the piecework. The quilting may be the main focus of the quilt, as in *The Sampler* (page 44).

The questions on the next page will help you focus your thoughts. You may read one question and right away know what type of quilting to use. But don't be surprised if you have to ask a couple questions to determine what is going to work for your quilt. Review the chapter dedicated to your quilt category to help you decide which quilting you want to use. Sometimes seeing an example will trigger an answer.

How important is the quilting to the quilt's overall impact?

When you look at the quilt top, does it look complete, or does it still need something? Quilts that have very little contrast in their design often look complete to me. When I see these types of quilts, I usually want to add simple quilting, like an allover design, as in *Oh So Sweet* (page 19). If the quilt has strong contrast in color and has some open spaces, I usually plan custom quilting, as in *Night in Avalon* (page 30) or *Mariner's Compass* (page 28).

Does the quilt need quilting to enhance it?

If your quilt has large areas without piecing, quilting will enhance these areas, especially if the fabrics are solid, as in *Chain Reaction* (page 29).

Is the quilt design so strong that the quilting needs to be simple?

If the design is the main focus, you do not want the quilting to draw attention away from the quilt (see *Hop City*, page 39).

Can the quilting help blend the quilt design and draw attention to its design elements?

Sometimes the quilting can reinforce a quilt design by following or accenting the piecework, as in *Midnight Sun* (page 38).

What fabrics were used in the quilt?

The fabric choices can have a big influence on the type of quilting you choose.

SOLID FABRICS

- Can showcase beautiful heirloom quilting

- Can have striking quilting with contrasting thread colors

- Can be frustrating to new quilters, because the fabrics show stitch length inconsistencies, poor thread stops and starts, and wobbly quilting lines

LARGE PRINTS

- Are good for allover quilting designs

- Can lend themselves to outline quilting using the designs on the fabric

- Are good for hiding any stitch length inconsistencies, poor thread stops and starts, and any wobbly quilting lines

SMALL/TINY PRINTS

- Are good for allover quilting designs

- Are good for beginning quilters, because the prints help hide any flaws in the quilting

- Are not good for custom quilting, because they make it difficult to see the quilting designs

Look at the examples in this book to help you make your quilting choices.

STEP 4
Select a Thread Color

Last, but Not Least

Choosing your thread color may be the last decision you make before you start quilting, but it is just as important as all the other decisions you have made thus far. Choosing the wrong thread color can detract from the overall esthetics of the quilt. Your quilting should never be a distraction and should always be in balance with the piecework. Many times, the design and piecework are the quilt's main focus, and the quilting is a complement.

For most quilts, choosing a matching thread color is your best choice.

Even the best quilting choices can look bad if the wrong thread color is chosen. The two images below are from the same quilt. I quilted each half of the quilt with a different thread to show how dramatically thread choices affect the look of a quilt. This quilt is a colorwash, and the intended design is for the quilt center to blend and, as your eye moves away from the center, for the blocks to appear.

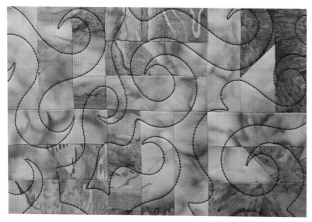

Poor thread choice: The dark thread is a distraction and takes away from the soft effect intended in the quilt center.

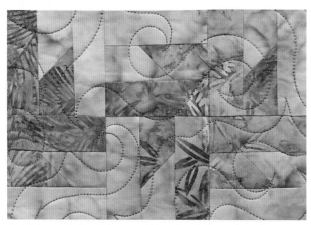

Good thread choice: Using a matching thread allows the quilting to blend with the quilt and the colorwash design element to be the quilt's main focus.

You might have a favorite thread in mind, but be open to seeing other options when you get to this point. A good hint is to unravel some thread from your spool and lay the strands on your quilt. Place all the colors of thread that you are considering on the quilt at the same time and see which looks best to you.

For a quilt that was going to have an allover quilting design, three thread options (below) were tested. I wanted the design to show and add a little interest to the quilt, but not be overwhelming. My choice was the variegated thread (top photo).

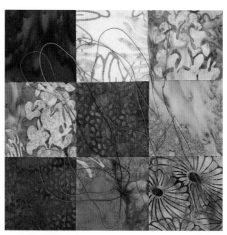

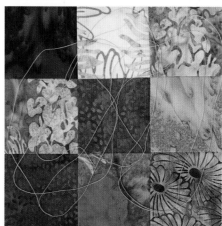

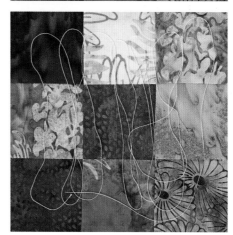

Three thread options

Not everyone will have an instinct regarding thread color. The guidelines on the next page will help you choose the best thread color.

MATCHING THREAD COLOR TO THE FABRIC

- Is your best choice when you are unsure

- Will help hide any inconsistencies in stitch length

- Can help hide thread stops and starts

- Allows the quilting to fade into the background

- Is my preferred choice for edgestitching on raw-edge appliqué

- Is good for adding texture or contour lines

- Is best when the quilting is intended to have a blending effect on the quilt

CONTRASTING THREAD COLOR WITH FABRIC COLORS

- Works well when you want the quilting to be the quilt's main focus

- Is used for thread painting

- Will showcase good stitch length consistency

VARIEGATED THREAD

- Is used for allover designs

- Shows off the quilting when used on solid fabrics

- Works well on bright, busy fabrics

- Is good on fabrics with large prints

- Shows inconsistency in stitch length and stitch tension when used on solid fabrics

GENERAL RULES OF THUMB

- With light fabrics, use light thread.

- With dark fabrics, use dark thread.

- Quilts with light, medium, and dark fabrics usually look best with a thread most closely matched to the midtone fabrics.

- If the quilt has strong color contrast, match your thread to the light fabric.

When quilting, I always match the thread color of the bobbin and top thread. This is a consideration you should keep in mind when choosing the color of your backing fabric.

Types of Thread

Thread is available in many fibers, including cotton, polyester, silk, rayon, poly/cotton blends, and wool. Even with all these choices, I prefer to use cotton thread because all the other materials in my quilts are cotton. I prefer long-stable Egyptian cotton threads, such as Aurifil Mako cotton. Every machine has its own idiosyncrasies, so don't be surprised if the threads that work best for you and your machine are not the same as for someone else. Try the threads that are available to you, and choose the ones that you like best. Tension adjustments often have to be made when changing between different thread manufacturers, even if the thread weight is the same.

I primarily use Aurifil cotton thread in two weights. I use the 28 weight for edgestitching appliqué and for quilting. I use Aurifil 40 weight for quilting that will be dense and close together. I also use 40 weight for my bobbins because of how much thread I can wind on a bobbin. Even when I am using 28 weight in the top thread, I use the 40-weight thread in the bobbin.

Children's/Youth Quilts

All the quilts in this chapter are for children or are inspired by children. Some of these quilts are going to be used as bed quilts, while others were made as pattern samples or for a magazine. You can see where the quilting choices varied depending on the use of the quilt. In most cases, quilts in this category have a more simplistic approach. Simple pattern designs are often used for children's quilts because of the amount of use these quilts receive. I've included examples of simple allover designs, partial custom quilting, and full custom quilting.

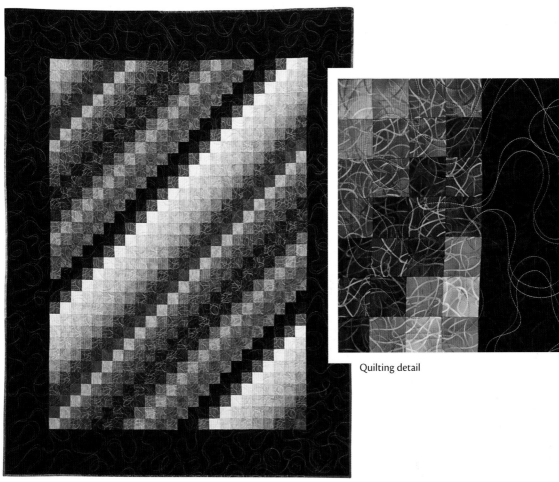

Quilting detail

Oh So Sweet, 62" × 79", designed by Barbara Persing and Mary Hoover, pieced by Mary Hoover, machine quilted by Barbara Persing

Pattern available at www.4and6designs.com.

Oh So Sweet

What is the intended use of the quilt?

This is a youth bed quilt. It was also used as a sample for our pattern *Oh So Sweet*.

What quilting is needed to enhance the quilt?

I wanted the quilting to blend with the quilt and not detract from the quilt design. The diagonal movement of the bold fabric colors dominates this quilt's focus. I used the fabric's ribbon motif as my inspiration for the quilting. This is an allover quilting design.

What thread color should I use?

I chose a variegated thread that would blend with the center of the quilt but would contrast with the black border. Since this was an allover design, using this thread on the border brought color from the quilt center into the border and highlighted the fabric's ribbon design.

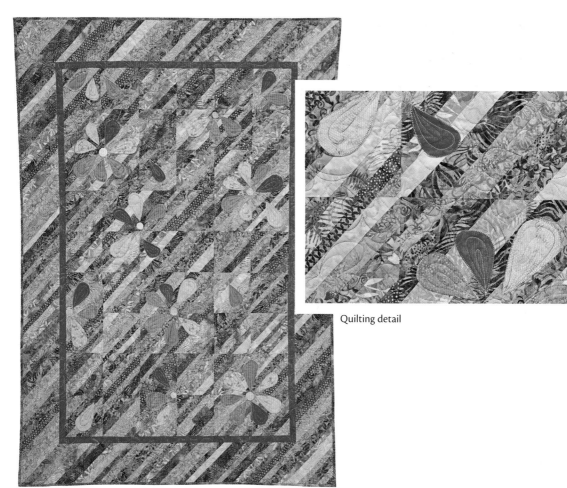

May Day, 47″ × 69″, designed and pieced by Barbara Persing
and Mary Hoover, machine quilted by Barbara Persing

Quilting detail

May Day

What is the intended use of the quilt?

This is a child's bed quilt. It was used as our sample quilt in our booth at International Quilt Festival, Houston, Texas.

What quilting is needed to enhance the quilt?

The shape of the appliqué flowers was the inspiration for the allover quilting design, and the impact of the strata background was not lost with this quilting approach. The allover quilting design will hold up well with frequent use and laundering. I was able to quilt this as a continuous line design without any stops. This is partial custom quilting.

What thread color should I use?

I chose a variegated pink thread to blend into the background and match the color of the flower petals.

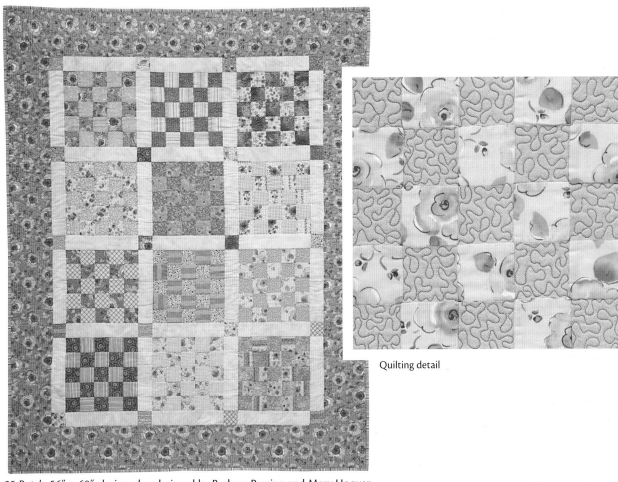

25-Patch, 56″ × 68″, designed and pieced by Barbara Persing and Mary Hoover, machine quilted by Barbara Persing

This pattern is available at www.4and6designs.com.

Quilting detail

25-Patch

What is the intended use of the quilt?

This is a bed quilt that was used as a pattern sample. I quilted this as if it were going to be used every day.

What quilting is needed to enhance the quilt?

The *25-Patch* blocks did not need much quilting. As for the border, the pink floral fabric would hide any detailed quilting, so I kept it simple. I chose stippling in the border and in every other block in the 25-patches. This is partial custom quilting.

What thread color should I use?

I choose a dark pink thread that matched the border and also went well with the other fabric in the quilt.

Quilting detail

This quilt was featured in *McCall's Quick Quilts*. The pattern and kit are available at www.ladyfingerssewing.com.

The Very Snuggly Story Time, 46" × 64", designed and pieced by Gail Kessler, machine quilted by Barbara Persing

The Very Snuggly Story Time

What is the intended use of the quilt?

This is a baby quilt that was featured in *McCall's Quick Quilts*. The quilting approach was intentionally developed as a custom design.

What quilting is needed to enhance the quilt?

Andover Fabrics commissioned my services. They wanted the quilting to be custom and to showcase the fabric. I did outline quilting on the large center leaf, butterfly, and caterpillar. I used the marble motif from the center fabric to create the small circles.

Comparing *The Very Hungry Caterpillar* (next page) and *The Very Snuggly Story Time*, you can see how quilting can make quilts look different. *The Very Snuggly Story Time* was quilted as full custom quilting, whereas the first version of this quilt, *The Very Hungry Caterpillar*, was quilted with an allover design. *This is an example of how the intended use of the quilt can affect your quilting choices.*

What thread color should I use?

I did not want the thread to be distracting, so I used ivory thread throughout the quilt.

Quilting detail

The Very Hungry Caterpillar, 46″ × 64″, designed by Gail Kessler, pieced and machine quilted by Barbara Persing

Fabric by Andover Fabrics; kit available at www.ladyfingerssewing.com.

The Very Hungry Caterpillar

What is the intended use of the quilt?

This quilt was a gift for a new baby.

What quilting is needed to enhance the quilt?

The fabric designs are the quilt's main focus. Because I did not want to detract from the fabric, I chose a very simple loop design. This quilting is also dense enough to handle frequent use and laundering. This is an allover design.

What thread color should I use?

Ivory thread was used because it does not detract from the quilt design.

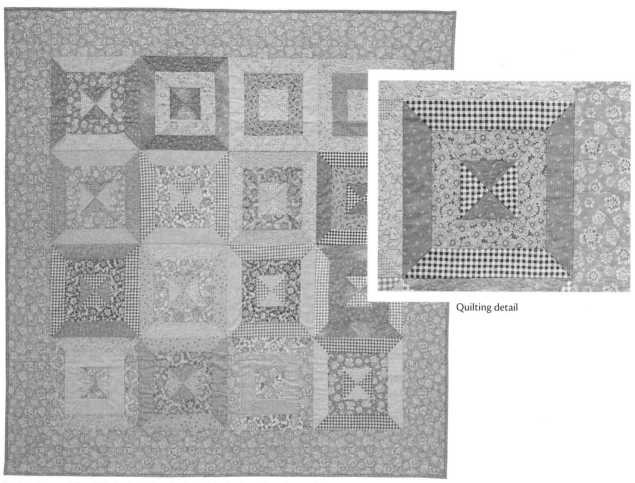

Quilting detail

Spring Fever, 48″ × 60″, designed and pieced by Barbara Persing and Mary Hoover, machine quilted by Barbara Persing

This pattern is available at www.4and6designs.com.

Spring Fever

What is the intended use of the quilt?

This a bed quilt that was created as a pattern sample.

What quilting is needed to enhance the quilt?

Many of the fabrics in this quilt have flowers, so I used that as my inspiration for the quilting. The border is quilted with a loop and daisy design. In the center of each block, I quilted a daisy. The alternating strips around each block were quilted using loops. This is an example of how one quilting design—the border—can be taken apart and used in other areas of the quilt, creating a comprehensive approach that ties the quilt together. This is partial custom quilting.

What thread color should I use?

I chose a medium yellow thread that blended well with all the fabrics in the quilt.

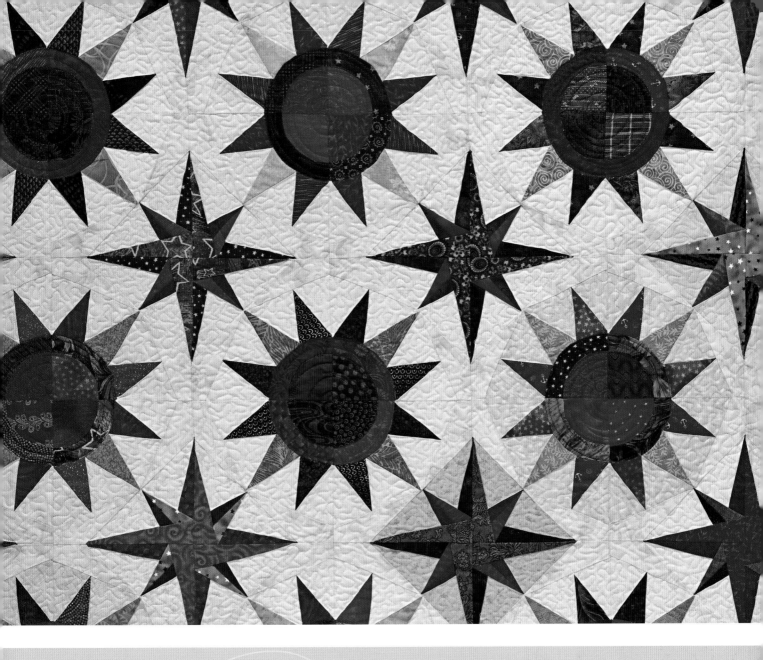

Traditional Quilts

All the quilts in this chapter are in the category of traditional quilts. There are many uses for these quilts and a variety of quilting approaches. Because these quilts are traditional, I tend to think about quilting designs such as feathers, stippling, crosshatching, or outlining. It is important to use more traditional quilting designs, because they will best complement the quilt. Think about what type of hand quilting might have been used on the quilt and try to adapt one of the designs from that technique. Look at the fabrics used in the quilt to see if a design there inspires you.

Quilting detail

Blue, 78" × 92", designed and pieced by Mary Hoover and Barbara Persing, machine quilted by Barbara Persing

Blue

What is the intended use of the quilt?

This is a bed quilt.

What quilting is needed to enhance the quilt?

This basic traditional quilt provided an opportunity for me to use quilting as a subtle additional design element. Because there are no open areas for custom quilting, the batik fabrics and small squares make this a good choice for an allover quilting design. I chose a circular design to contrast with the squares; the blue color of the fabric inspired the watery, wavelike motif.

What thread color should I use?

I chose a variegated thread of red, blue, purple, and gold that would allow the quilting's watery design to be another focal point on the quilt. This contrasting color provided a complementary dimension in addition to the squares and the circular quilting.

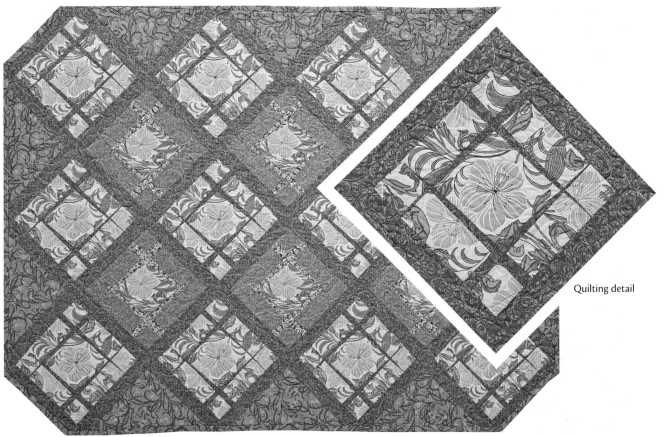

Quilting detail

Bliss, 54″ × 73″, pieced by Nancy Cosmos,
machine quilted by Barbara Persing, pattern by Lisa O'Neill

The pattern is available in the book *Sliver Quilts* by Lisa O'Neill,
published by C&T Publishing.

Bliss

What is the intended use of the quilt?

This is a bed quilt.

What quilting is needed to enhance the quilt?

The overall attractiveness of this quilt did not call for elaborate
custom quilting. The flowers in the center block designs, the
piecework, and the soft fabric shades create a complete pre-
sentation. I therefore wanted the quilting to be subtle and to
not take attention away from the quilt design. I used the leafy
pattern in one of the fabrics as the inspiration for the allover
quilting design. I highlighted the flowers in the center of the
blocks with outline quilting. This is partial custom quilting.

What thread color should I use?

I used a neutral ivory thread so the quilting would
blend with the quilt fabrics.

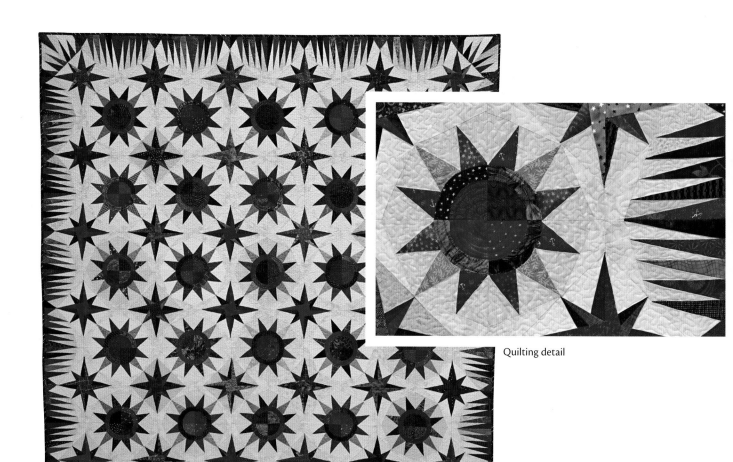

Quilting detail

Mariner's Compass, 74″ × 74″, pieced by Karen Darin,
machine quilted by Barbara Persing, pattern by Judy Niemeyer

Mariner's Compass

What is the intended use of the quilt?

This is a wall quilt.

What quilting is needed to enhance the quilt?

The quilt has strong color contrast, and the stars are its main
focus. This quilt was pieced using a paper-piecing technique,
and the cream background has many seams. Therefore,
the background needed to be quilted simply so it would
not draw attention away from the stars. I chose an allover
stippling to help the cream fabric appear to be one piece

of fabric. Because the stars are the quilt's main focus, I
highlighted the star centers by quilting them in circles
and left all the star points unquilted, allowing them to
stand out. Similarly, I left all the points along the border
unquilted. This is full custom quilting.

What thread color should I use?

The background was quilted using matching ivory thread,
and the stars were quilted using matching red thread.

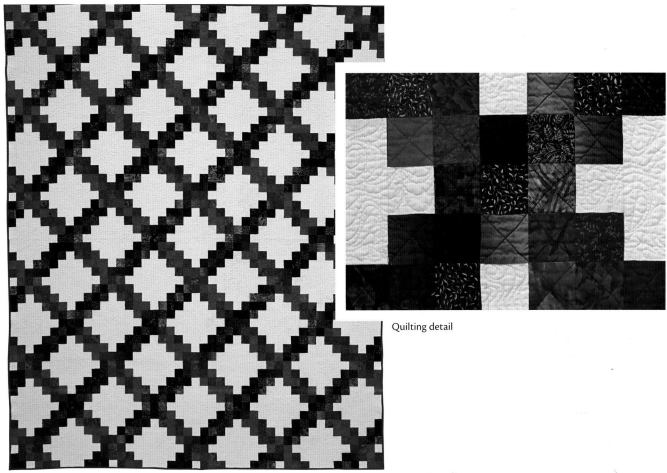

Quilting detail

Chain Reaction, 90″ × 110″, designed by Barbara Persing and Mary Hoover, pieced by Mary Hoover, machine quilted by Barbara Persing

Pattern available at www.4and6designs.com.

Chain Reaction

What is the intended use of the quilt?

This is a bed quilt that was also used as a pattern sample.

What quilting is needed to enhance the quilt?

Because this quilt has large, open white spaces, detailed quilting needed to be added. I quilted the diagonal chain of squares with soft curvy crosshatching. Because I quilt on a longarm and do not like to use a ruler, I always use a soft, curvy line for crosshatching. This is full custom quilting.

What thread color should I use?

I did not want to make the white area distracting, so I used a matching ivory thread. In the red and blue chain, I used a variegated thread of matching blue, red, and gold.

Night in Avalon, 54" × 54", pieced by Barbara Kenny, machine quilted by Barbara Persing

Pattern published by Fons & Porter's *Love of Quilting*, September/October 2008.

Quilting detail

Night in Avalon

What is the intended use of the quilt?

This is a wall quilt.

What quilting is needed to enhance the quilt?

This quilt's focal point is the center star and the contrasting colors of the fabrics. Although all the spaces were filled with different quilting designs, all the designs have a common curved theme that was inspired by the motifs on the border fabric. When you look at the back of the quilt, you can clearly see all the quilting designs used. This is full custom quilting.

What thread color should I use?

I chose matching red and green threads, as it was important for the quilting to be subtle to let the star remain the quilt's main focus. Even though I used matching thread colors, the quilting becomes apparent when viewed as a wallhanging and adds a complementary dimension to the quilt.

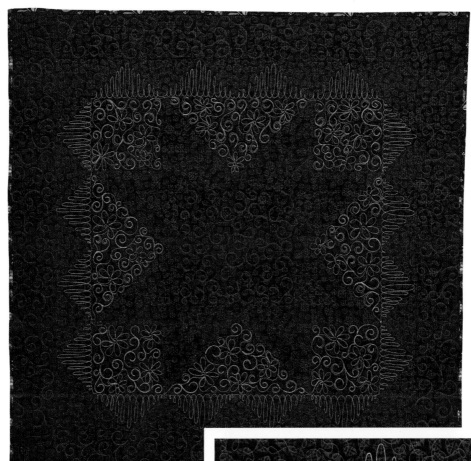

Quilt back, *Night in Avalon*

Quilt back, quilting detail

Quilting detail 1

Birdhouse, 75" × 77", designed and pieced by Laura Roberts, machine quilted by Barbara Persing

Birdhouse

What is the intended use of the quilt?

This is a wallhanging.

What quilting is needed to enhance the quilt?

This quilt was made with very soft, muted fabrics and no strong design elements. Since this quilt was going to be displayed on a wall, it needed to have focal interest to draw in the viewer and keep the viewer interested. The quilting was designed around the spaces provided by the piecework—a soft curvy, complementary design was used. The quilting did not need to be dramatic; rather it had to fill the quilt with texture and interest.

What thread color should I use?

Matching thread color was used throughout the quilt so the quilting would create texture without taking away from the quilt's soft appearance.

Quilting detail 2, blocks

Quilting detail 4, borders

Quilting detail 3

Quilting detail 5, inner border

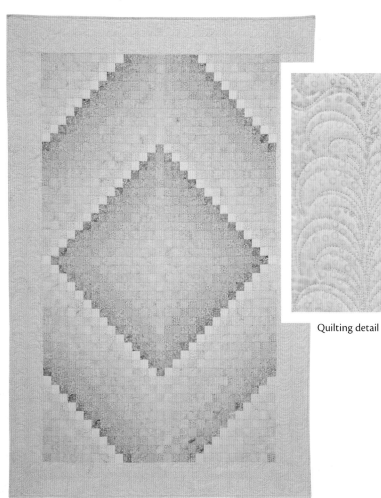

Quilting detail

Trip Around the World, 49″ × 76″, pieced by Mary Hoover,
machine quilted by Barbara Persing, pattern by Piecemakers

Pattern and kit available at www.4and6designs.com.

Trip Around the World

What is the intended use of the quilt?

This is a throw quilt. It was made as a sample for our kits
and was displayed in our booth at International Quilt
Festival, Houston, Texas.

What quilting is needed to enhance the quilt?

Because this quilt is a soft colorwash, we did not want the
quilting to be overwhelming, but we did want the quilt
to have an heirloom appearance. Each square was quilted

with tight squiggles (page 66). In alternating squares,
the line direction changed, which emphasizes the
detailed block piecing. A fern design was used to quilt
the ivory border to contrast with the square design in
the quilt center (page 64). This is full custom quilting.

What thread color should I use?

Matching ivory thread was used so the quilting would
blend and not detract from the quilt's colorwash effect.

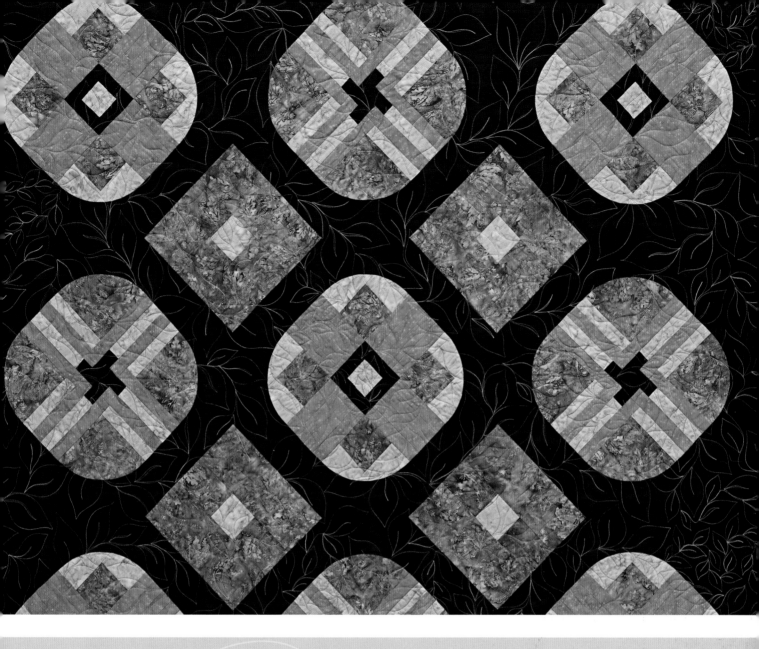

Contemporary Quilts

All the quilts in this chapter are contemporary. What I like most about quilts in this category is that you can use your current quilting designs but apply them in a different way or slightly change them. For example, if you like to quilt feathers, use them on contemporary quilts but make them less uniform—let them flow naturally around the quilt and onto the borders. Quilt them without measuring and drawing the spines. Quilt them free motion and have fun with it. Contemporary quilts are an opportunity to be unconventional and to build your creative free-motion quilting skills.

Quilting detail

Flower Pots, 88″ × 97″, pieced by Janet Street, machine quilted by Barbara Persing, pattern by Kim McLean

Flower Pots

What is the intended use of the quilt?

This is a bed quilt.

What quilting is needed to enhance the quilt?

This quilt was beautifully hand appliquéd by Janet Street. She chose large, bold prints for her fabrics, which gives this quilt its contemporary feel. Janet had a clear vision for her quilt and wanted to be unconventional in her quilting choices, choosing to have an allover design. The quilting motifs are simple, whimsical, and flowing to complement the fabrics used.

What thread color should I use?

Because the quilting on this was going to be an allover design, even across the appliqué, a variegated thread was chosen to carry the colors of the appliqué across the quilt. The background fabric was not a solid; it had a small design, and that helped make this thread choice work perfectly.

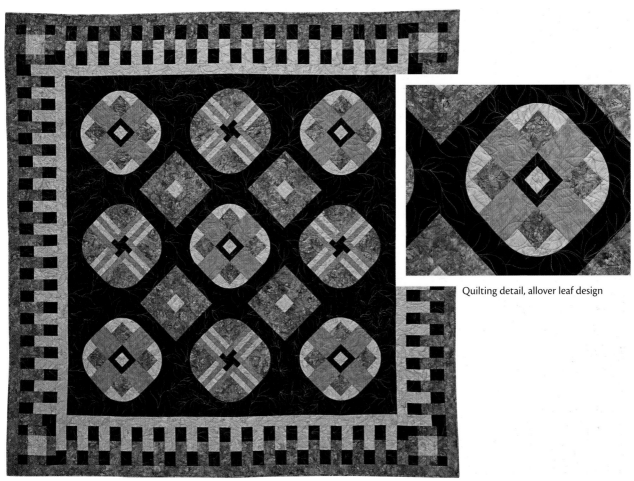

Quilting detail, allover leaf design

Katrina's Quilt, 85″ × 85″, designed and pieced by Gina Guaraldi, machine quilted by Barbara Persing

Pattern available at Bitty Kinna's Quilt Shop, Intercourse, Pennsylvania.

Katrina's Quilt

What is the intended use of the quilt?

This is a bed quilt. It was also used as a pattern sample.

What quilting is needed to enhance the quilt?

With this quilt's sharp contrasting colors, the solid black fabric for the background appeared stark. The black background fabric needed a quilting design that would help it blend with the rest of the quilt. The leaf design was inspired by the quilt fabric. This is an allover design.

What thread color should I use?

The black fabric needed to have a visible design added, so a variegated green thread was used in an allover quilting design. The designer of this quilt wanted the quilting on the black background to show so the black would look less austere. This is a good example of how to change the look of a fabric choice with a contrasting thread.

Quilting detail

Midnight Sun, 55" × 77", pieced by Teresa Riden,
machine quilted by Barbara Persing, designed by Jinny Beyer

Pattern in Fons & Porter's *Love of Quilting*, November/December 2008 issue.

Midnight Sun

What is the intended use of the quilt?

This is a throw quilt.

What quilting is needed to enhance the quilt?

This quilt is a colorwash of batik fabrics. The gradual
change of color and the strata design are the quilt's
main focus. I used the strata as a guide for the quilting
to further accent the quilt design. The quilting motif in
the border was inspired by fabric used in the quilt.

What thread color should I use?

I chose a variegated thread that worked with all the
colors found in the quilt. Sometimes it is difficult
to choose a thread color when the colors change
throughout the quilt. Often the best choice is a
variegated thread. The color of this thread matched
the midtones of the fabrics used—it was not too light
and not too dark.

Quilting detail

Hop City, 47″ × 52″, designed and pieced by Barbara Persing and Mary Hoover, machine quilted by Barbara Persing

Pattern published in *StrataVarious Quilts*, by Barbara Persing and Mary Hoover (C&T Publishing); available at www.4and6designs.com.

Hop City

What is the intended use of the quilt?

This quilt is a wallhanging. It was designed as a pattern for our book *StrataVarious Quilts*.

What quilting is needed to enhance the quilt?

The geometric design of the purple and orange squares, as well as the strong color contrast, are this quilt's main focus. I wanted the quilting to blend with the background but have some reference to the quilt design. I created a geometric design that was off balance, similar to the tilting block in the quilt. The quilting is a continuous line design. This is partial custom quilting.

What thread color should I use?

Matching thread colors were used to blend the quilting so it would not detract from the quilt design. Peach thread was used on the background, and orange thread was used on the large orange squares.

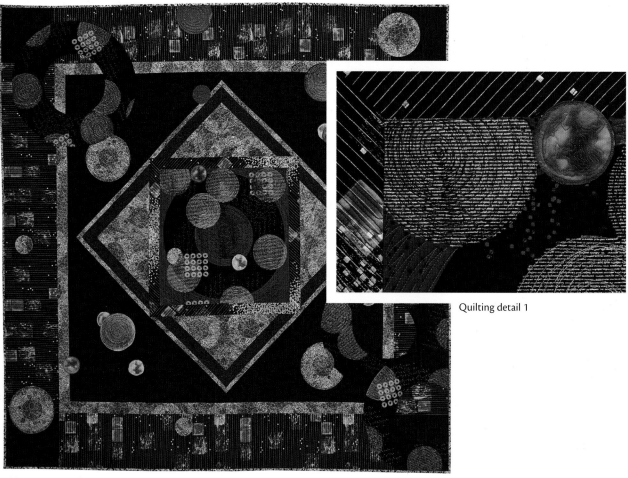

Chloe's Quilt, 80" × 80", designed and pieced by Mary Hoover, machine quilted by Barbara Persing

Quilting detail 1

Chloe's Quilt

What is the intended use of the quilt?

This quilt is a wallhanging that was going to be used as a show quilt.

What quilting is needed to enhance the quilt?

The inspiration for this quilt started with the fabrics. The primary focus of this quilt is in the design—the large on-point squares and the floating circle designs. Because this quilt was going to be entered into a show, the quilting needed to be as interesting and as well done as the quilt. All the quilting designs were inspired by the appliqué and the motifs of the fabrics used in the quilt. This gave the quilting a direct correlation to the quilt's circular theme. What first attracts you to this quilt is the strong design; then, as you move closer to the quilt, the quilting becomes obvious. This is heirloom quilting.

What thread color should I use?

Many thread colors were used, each matching the fabrics where the quilting was done. Thread colors were black, grays, steel blue, and brown.

Quilting detail 2

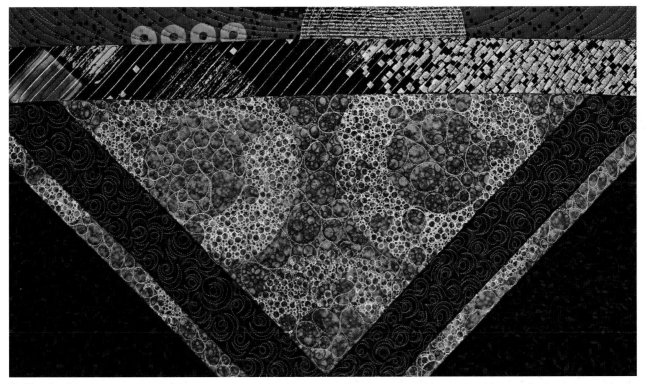

Quilting detail 3

Quilting detail 1

Country Blessings, 94" × 94", pieced by Gail Kessler,
machine quilted by Barbara Persing, pattern by Nancy Murty

Country Blessings

What is the intended use of the quilt?

This is a bed quilt that was also a shop sample.

What quilting is needed to enhance the quilt?

This pattern is usually appliquéd with a more traditional
group of fabrics, but Gail Kessler put her own touch on this
quilt by using jewel-tone fabrics for the appliqué. The choices
she made for the fabrics inspired me to use a less traditional
approach for the quilting. I used many whimsical designs and a
less traditional background fill. I used the shape and curves of
the appliqué to design small quilting motifs to fill each space.

What thread color should I use?

Matching thread colors were used to match all the fabrics,
and a matching ivory thread was used on the background.
Because the appliqué is this quilt's main focus, adding a
contrasting thread would have been very distracting.

Quilting detail 2

Quilting detail 3

Quilting detail 4

The Sampler, 67" × 81", designed and pieced by Barbara Persing, machine quilted by Barbara Persing

This quilt won Best Machine Workmanship, 2009, Pennsylvania National Quilt Extravaganza.

Quilting detail 1

The Sampler

What is the intended use of the quilt?

This quilt is a wallhanging. It was designed to be a show quilt and to specifically showcase the quilting designs.

What quilting is needed to enhance the quilt?

Solid fabrics were used in this quilt so that all the quilting designs would become the main focus. All the quilting in the quilt center was spontaneous. I wanted to show many different types of quilting motifs and how they can all work together on the same quilt. Because this quilt is contemporary, I chose to quilt each background area and each circle design differently. Had I used more traditional colors and fabric, I would have quilted this much differently (see the quilting comparison, page 12). The border was marked with a 1" grid that was set on point, and that served as a guide for the three quilting designs in the border. I freehand quilted the corner feather designs.

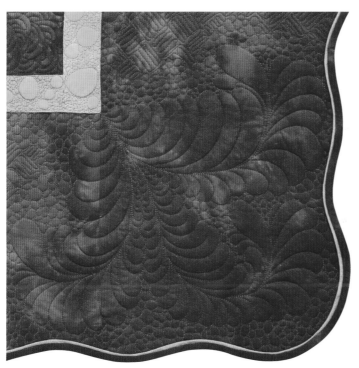

Quilting detail 2, corner feather design

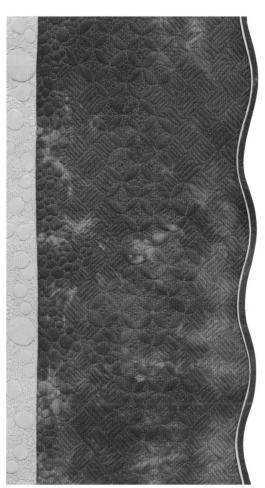

Quilting detail 3, border designs

What thread color should I use?

Because all the fabrics used in this quilt were solids, the quilting would really show. Because I was going to use so many different quilting motifs, I chose to match the threads to the fabrics. All the quilting was done with Aurifil 40-weight cotton because of its high sheen and because of how beautiful it looks on the hand-dyed solid cottons.

Quilting detail 4, *The Sampler*

Quilting detail 5

Art Quilts

All the quilts in this chapter are art quilts. This does not mean that the quilting is the most important part of the quilt. The quilting may be a significant part of the quilt and give it the final definition that it needs. Or the quilting may support the intended focus of the quilt. As with the other categories, you must closely evaluate the role of the quilting in the finished piece.

Quilts in this category often are pictorial and will need quilting that depicts the texture of the object. This type of quilting can be easy because you are not trying to repeat a specific shape over and over again; rather, you are adding random lines as a reference for the shape.

Many resources are available that show the types of textures or lines you could add to the quilt. Books with examples of nature, people, or shapes done as pencil drawings can help you visualize quilting lines. Also, search online for the image you need help with and look at photos of the actual object to get quilting ideas.

Into the Misty, 33″ × 42″, designed, appliquéd, and machine quilted by Barbara Persing

Quilting detail

Into the Misty

What is the intended use of the quilt?

This is a show quilt and wallhanging.

What quilting is needed to enhance the quilt?

Because this quilt is pictorial, many of the design elements—such as the texture on the trees, the definition in the background, and the mist going across the quilt—needed to be added with the quilting. Also, the appliqué on this quilt was done using a raw-edge appliqué technique that required edge stitching as I quilted. All of these elements are essential to the finished quilt and could only be added with quilting.

What thread color should I use?

I used matching thread for the appliqué edge stitching, the texture on the trees, and the background. The mist was added using a contrasting ivory thread.

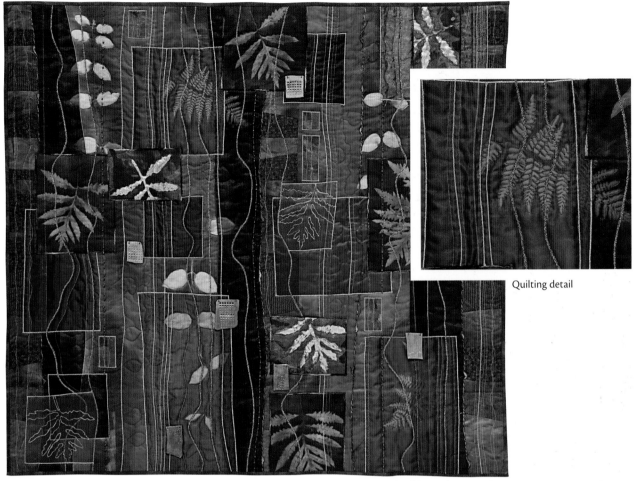

Quilting detail

Large Blue Silver Fern, 53" × 49", designed and pieced by Diane Bielak, machine quilted by Barbara Persing.

Large Blue Silver Fern

What is the intended use of the quilt?

This is a wall quilt by Diane Bielak, a professional fiber artist. Her quilts are for exhibit and for purchase.

What quilting is needed to enhance the quilt?

Diane and I have collaborated on many projects. Sometimes she will direct me in the type of quilting she wants, and sometimes she will leave it up to me. On this quilt, she wanted subtle vertical quilting lines and outlining of the painted fern motifs. Diane often will embellish her quilts after the quilting. It is important to add the embellishments after the quilting because they can get in the way of the quilting lines or even cause the needle to break while quilting—and possibly damage the quilt.

What thread color should I use?

I used a matching thread so the quilting would not be distracting and would only add the necessary texture.

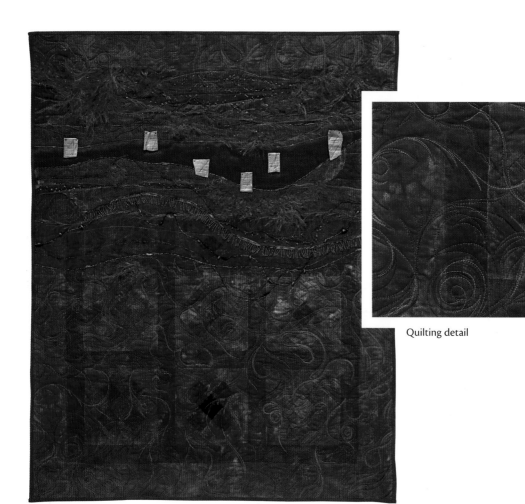

Red Sea, 40″ × 50″, designed and pieced by Diane Bielak,
machine quilted by Barbara Persing

Quilting detail

Red Sea

What is the intended use of the quilt?

This is a wall quilt by Diane Bielak, a professional fiber artist. Her quilts are for exhibit and for purchase.

What quilting is needed to enhance the quilt?

This quilt was a challenge from Diane to me. She was experimenting with different techniques, and she left the quilting ideas to me. I decided to use an allover design that I felt was organic. I knew she would embellish this quilt, and I was hoping the quilting would leave many avenues open for interpretation.

What thread color should I use?

This quilt was monochromatic, so I decided to use a contrasting variegated blue thread. I knew this thread choice would add interest to the quilt, as well as provide an element of challenge to Diane as to how she would finish the quilt.

Diane was pleasantly surprised when I returned the quilt to her. She said I really rose to the challenge, and now she was stumped. After some contemplation, she finished the quilt and entered it into a quilt show, where it won third place.

Quilting detail

This quilt was entered into Quilt Odyssey 2005 in Hershey, Pennsylvania, and won Best Pictorial by Machine.

September, 41″ × 33″, designed and appliquéd by Mary Hoover, machine quilted by Barbara Persing

September

What is the intended use of the quilt?

This quilt is a wallhanging. It was originally made to be a show quilt.

What quilting is needed to enhance the quilt?

The fabrics for this quilt were hand painted by Mary Hoover. The raw-edge appliqué flowers and the background needed added texture and detail, and all the appliqué needed to be edgestitched as I quilted. Because the fabric was so beautiful and perfect for the flowers, I used the designs created by the changing color as my quilting guide. To the stems and leaves I added the appropriate texture lines that you see in these

objects. The solid purple background was the perfect complement to the colors of the flowers, and I wanted the flowers to remain the quilt's main focus. I quilted the background with a soft, echoing quilting fill.

What thread color should I use?

I chose matching thread colors for the flowers. I used 24 different thread colors of yellows, browns, greens, and purples. I quilted the background with a variety of purple threads—not a variegated thread. The change of color in a variegated thread was too frequent, and I wanted to control where the color changes occurred.

Yellow Daisies, 36″ × 36″, designed, appliquéd, and machine quilted by Barbara Persing

Quilting detail

Yellow Daisies

What is the intended use of the quilt?

This wall quilt was commissioned by Aurifil Thread for its booth at International Quilt Market in Houston, Texas.

What quilting is needed to enhance the quilt?

For the appliqué flowers, I used one piece of fabric for each flower. I planned to add all the details to the flowers and stems with the quilting lines. The flowers were raw-edge appliqué and needed to be edgestitched as I quilted. The background was quilted with a free-motion fill of leaves, stones, and flowers that correlated to the quilt's theme and added a subtle secondary design element.

Quilt back, quilting detail

Quilt back, *Yellow Daisies*

What thread color should I use?

I always use a matching thread color for appliqué edge stitching. I then added additional thread colors to the flowers for texture and detail. The impression of each flower petal was added with simple quilting lines; it does not take an extraordinary amount of quilting to create texture on an object in a quilt. The background was quilted with a purple variegated thread to make the quilting design more visible. I used two weights of Aurifil thread for the quilting—Aurifil 28 weight for the appliqué edge stitching and Aurifil 40 weight for all of the quilting.

Quilting detail 1

Tulip, 44" × 62", designed, painted, and machine quilted by Barbara Persing

Tulip

What is the intended use of the quilt?
This is a show quilt and wallhanging.

What quilting is needed to enhance the quilt?
This quilt is a painted whole cloth. All the definition and textures of the flower needed to be added with quilting lines. In the unquilted image, it was not clear where the flower petals overlapped and in which direction they were folded. This quilt came to life because of the quilting. The texture in the quilt center and the movement in the petals were created by the quilting.

What thread color should I use?
The purpose of the quilting was to support the original design. By matching the threads to the colors in the quilt, the quilting actually brings the quilt into focus. This is a good example of how even though the thread matches the quilt, the quilting still has an impact.

Quilting detail 2

Tulip, before quilting

Peony, 57″ × 57″, designed, painted, and quilted by Barbara Persing

Quilting detail 1, flower center

Peony

What is the intended use of the quilt?

This is a show quilt and wallhanging.

What quilting is needed to enhance the quilt?

This quilt is a painted whole cloth. I wanted the image to have dimension, and the quilting helped enhance this aspect of the quilt. By using the quilting as contour lines, I was able to show the flow of the petals and leaves. All the quilting was inspired by my photograph of a peony. I used the natural lines of the flower to create the quilting lines.

What thread color should I use?

Almost all the thread used in this quilt was matching. In a few places, I used a slightly darker thread to create depth and shadow in the flower where I felt the painted shadow was not dark enough.

Quilting detail 2, leaf

Quilting detail 3, use of dark thread

Quilting Designs

The following line drawings are continuous line designs. These examples show how you can adapt your doodles into quilting lines. All of these designs can be used on small or large areas. As you have seen in the previous chapters, mixing and matching a few designs can be the start of a custom quilt. Custom quilting usually requires many stops and starts with thread. However, if you plan well, you may be able to move from block to block with few thread stops and starts—that is, in a continuous line.

After hours, days, weeks, and years of quilting, you will find that certain designs feel the most natural to you, and your own personal style will emerge. I encourage you to create your own designs and embrace your uniqueness.

Continuous Line, Allover Designs

These continuous line designs can be used as an allover quilting design or to fill any area on a quilt. If you are going to use these quilting designs as an allover design, be sure to increase the scale of the design. If you are going to use the design as a fill design, then scale the size to fit your space. I also use these as border designs.

Doodle

Mazy

Loops and leaves

Spiral

Swirls

Vine

Bubbles

Start

Reverse

Ribbon

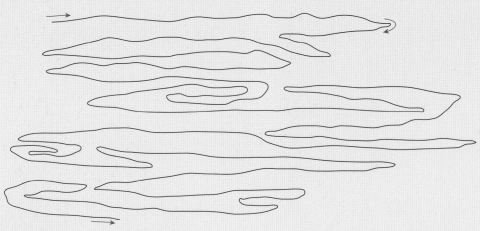

Wood texture

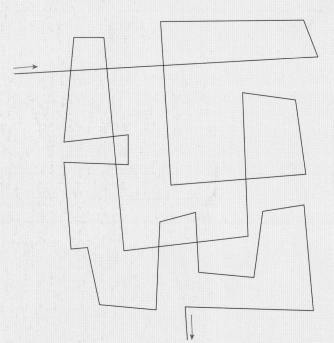

Modern art

Teardrops

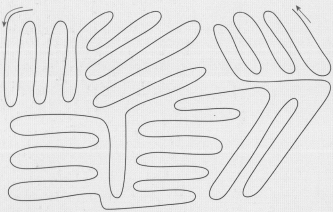

E and L

Change of direction

Cyclone

Arches

Stacking roses

Borders and Sashing

Borders and sashing often need a separate quilting design. There are many options to choose from, but I like continuous line designs. These designs can be easily scaled to fit your border or sashing with no redrawing or marking of the quilt. The following designs can be used in both borders and sashing and should be reduced or enlarged to fill the space.

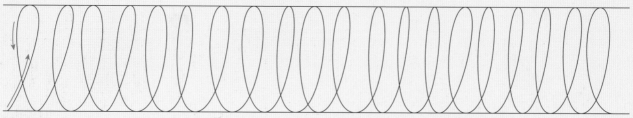

"L" design

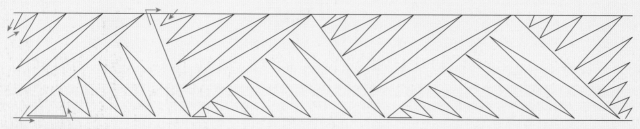

Zigzag

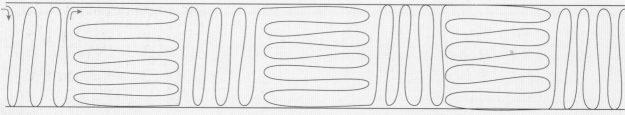

Squiggles

Fern

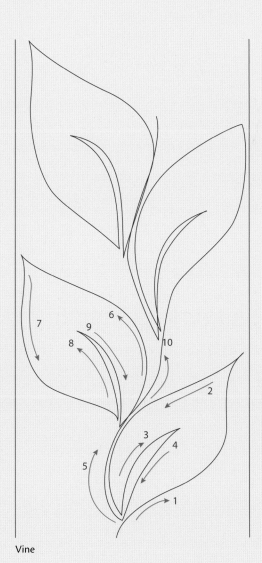

Vine

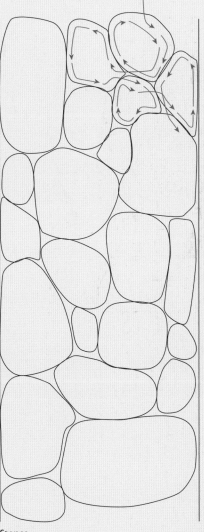

Stones

Squares

Many quilts are made using squares. The following quilting motifs can all be done as continuous line designs.

Ribbon

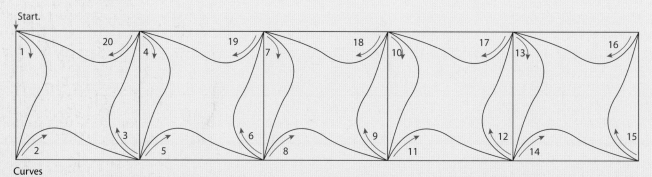

Curves

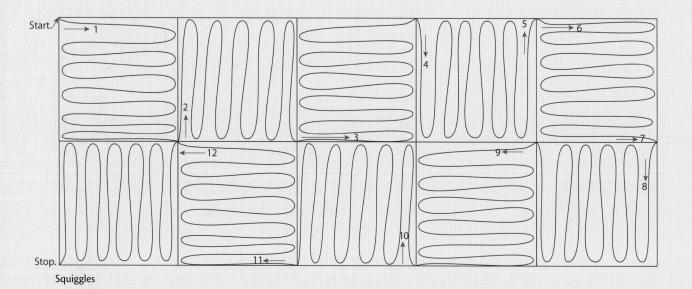

Squiggles

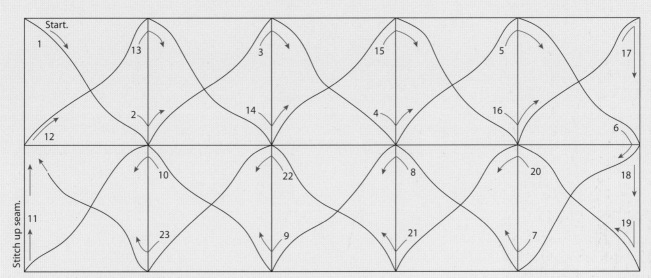

Wavy crosshatching: I like this design because it does not require the use of a ruler.

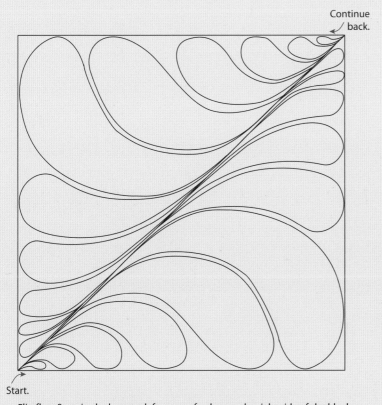

Flip flop: Start in the bottom left corner, feather up the right side of the block, and then come down the other side of the block.

Triangles can be found in many quilts. These designs will fill one or multiple triangles in a continuous line.

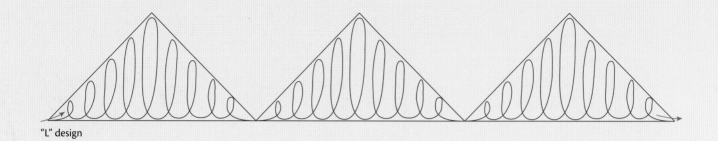

"L" design

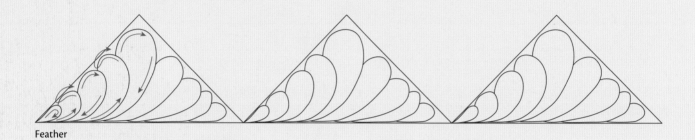

Feather

Leaves

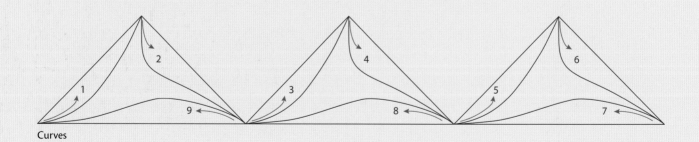

Curves

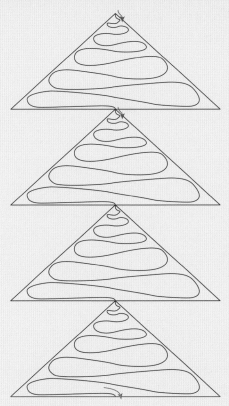

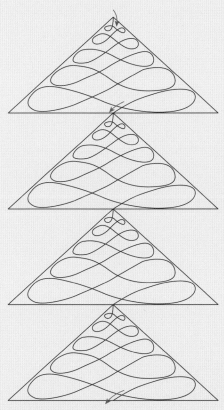

Triangle ribbons

Triangle eights

Tulips

Resources

Andover Fabrics, Inc.

www.andoverfabrics.com

1384 Broadway, Suite 1500

New York, NY 10018

212-710-1000

800-223-5678

Aurifil USA

www.aurifil.com

184 Shuman Boulevard, Suite 200

Naperville, IL 60563

312-212-3485

Bitty Kinna's

www.bittykinna.com

3466 Old Philadelphia Pike

Intercourse, PA 17534

717-768-8885

Fons & Porter's *Love of Quilting*

www.fonsandporter.com

1-888-985-1020

Glorious Color, Inc.

(*for Kim McLean patterns*)

www.gloriouscolor.com

800-269-0309

Nancy Murty

www.beecreativestudio.com

Bee Creative Studio

284 Ellsworth Road

Palmyra, NY 14522

315-597-1478

Judy Niemeyer Quilting

www.quiltworx.com

444 Margrethe Road

PO Box 5264

Kalispell, MT 59903

406-314-4340

Ladyfingers Sewing Studio

www.ladyfingerssewing.com

6375 Oley Turnpike Road

Oley, PA 19547

610-689-0068

Piecemakers

www.piecemakers.com

1720 Adams Avenue

Costa Mesa, CA 92626

714-641-3112

Rob Spring Photography

www.robspringphotography.com

Saratoga Springs, NY

518-584-0596

About the Author

Barbara Persing was born in New Jersey, where her mother taught her and her four sisters how to sew. This was the beginning of Barbara's love for sewing, but she did not learn about quilting until eight years later, when she and her mother took a quilting class. Her first quilt of traditional blocks was made using cardboard templates. Over the past 35 years, she has grown as a quilt designer—her quilts today look nothing like those first quilts she made with her mother.

Barbara now lives in Pennsylvania with her husband and two sons. She has always been a working mom but started working from home in 2000, when quilting went from being a hobby to a full-time job, and she started her own business as a longarm quilter. Her business quickly grew because her customers appreciated her unique ability to develop quilting designs to highlight the personality of their quilts. Her imagination for quilting designs grew as she worked for quilters with a wide variety of interests and styles. Barbara enjoys

the challenge of providing her customers with creative machine quilting designs that are as distinctive as the unique style of each customer. Embracing this challenge became the beginning of her quilting approach— "I work for the quilt." The most important aspect of her job is to marry the quilting to the style of the quilt.

She is thankful to her clients for giving her so much inspiration as a quilter. Barbara will tell you that each quilt she works on provides a new learning experience that enhances her abilities. She is amazed at what she can accomplish when pushed to work outside of her own comfort zone.

In 2006, Barbara again started a new venture. In addition to her longarm quilting business, she started a pattern company, Fourth & Sixth Designs, with her sister Mary Hoover. Mary lives in New York and shares Barbara's love of quilting. Their patterns have been featured in *Keepsake Quilting* and many other national quilting magazines. Together, Barbara and Mary wrote *StrataVarious Quilts*, published by C&T, and enjoy teaching and lecturing.

Despite a hectic schedule, Barbara continues to find time for her dedicated clients and enjoys every minute of collaboration with them. She still loves to spend all day running her longarm machine.

You can visit Barbara's website at www.barbarapersing.com and contact her at barb@barbarapersing.com.

Also by Barbara Persing:

Great Titles *from* C&T PUBLISHING

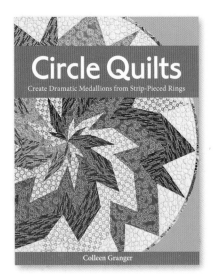

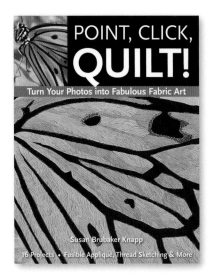

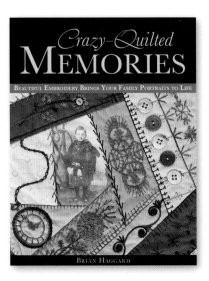

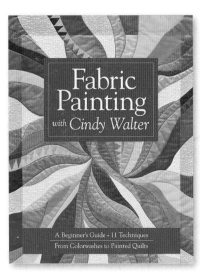

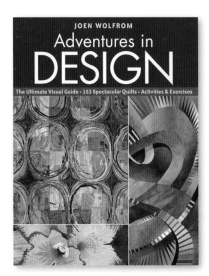

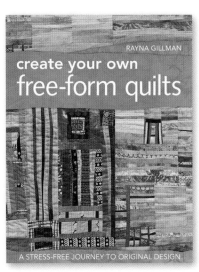

Available at your local retailer or **www.ctpub.com** *or* **800-284-1114**

For a list of other fine books from C&T Publishing, visit our website
to view our catalog online

C&T PUBLISHING, INC.

P.O. Box 1456
Lafayette, CA 94549
800-284-1114

Email: ctinfo@ctpub.com
Website: www.ctpub.com

C&T Publishing's professional photography services are now available to
the public. Visit us at www.ctmediaservices.com.

Tips and Techniques can be found at www.ctpub.com > Consumer
Resources > Quiltmaking Basics: Tips & Techniques for Quiltmaking & More

For quilting supplies:

COTTON PATCH

1025 Brown Ave.
Lafayette, CA 94549
Store: 925-284-1177
Mail order: 925-283-7883

Email: CottonPa@aol.com
Website: www.quiltusa.com

Note: Fabrics shown may not be currently available, as fabric
manufacturers keep most fabrics in print for only a short time.